Physical Fitness and Resilience

A Review of Relevant Constructs, Measures, and Links to Well-Being

Sean Robson

RAND Project AIR FORCE

Prepared for the United States Air Force
Approved for public release; distribution unlimited

- medical
- nutritional
- environmental
- physical
- social
- spiritual
- behavioral
- psychological.

These supplemental reports are not intended to be a comprehensive review of the entire literature within a domain. Rather, they focus on studies that consider the stress-buffering aspects of each domain, regardless of whether the term *resilience* is specifically used. This expanded the scope of the reviews to include a broader range of applicable studies and also allowed for terminology differences that occur across different disciplines (e.g., stress management, hardiness).

In this report, we identify key constructs relevant to physical fitness from the scientific literature: work-related physical fitness and health-related physical fitness. The domains include factors that increase an individual's ability to meet the physical demands of a specific job or job-related task as well as activities associated with improved health outcomes. This review includes construct measures as well as well-being and resilience outcomes. We also review interventions designed to promote physical fitness applicable at the individual, unit, family, and community levels.

The results of these reports should be relevant to Air Force leaders who are tasked with monitoring and supporting the well-being of active duty, reserve, and guard Airmen and Air force civilian employees, as well as their families. The results of our studies may also help broaden the scope of research on resilience and help Airmen and their families achieve optimal physical fitness.

The research described in this report was conducted within the Manpower, Personnel, and Training Program of RAND Project AIR FORCE as part of a fiscal year 2011 study titled "Program and Facility Support for Air Force Personnel and Family Resiliency."

RAND Project AIR FORCE

RAND Project AIR FORCE (PAF), a division of the RAND Corporation, is the U.S. Air Force's federally funded research and development center for studies and analyses. PAF provides the Air Force with independent analyses of policy alternatives affecting the development, employment, combat readiness, and support of current and future air, space, and cyber forces. Research is conducted in four programs: Force Modernization and Employment; Manpower, Personnel, and Training; Resource Management; and Strategy and Doctrine.

Additional information about PAF is available on our website:
http://www.rand.org/paf/

Contents

Summary

Physical fitness, as it relates to the concept of Total Force Fitness (TFF), is defined as a set of health or performance-related attributes relating to the activities and condition of the body. Key resilience factors, or constructs that are associated with successfully coping with stress and strain, include both work-related and health-related physical fitness. Work-related physical fitness activities are those that increase an individual's ability to meet the physical demands of a specific job or job-related task, whereas health-related activities are those associated with reduced morbidity, the onset of chronic conditions (e.g., high blood pressure, diabetes), and mortality.

In general, science is moving away from fitness standards based on population norms (e.g., percentiles) to those based on health-related outcomes. Thus, most of this report focuses on physical activity, given its importance for overall physical health. Physical activity can provide considerable benefits to both physical and mental health and can buffer the negative effects of stress. It is important to note that physical activity includes more than aerobic activities. It can also include such activities as walking, yoga, bowling, dancing, and gardening, and these activities can be very beneficial for sedentary, injured/ill, obese, and exercise-averse populations. In fact, those who are less fit may see even greater benefits from physical activity than those who are more fit.

Interventions to promote physical fitness are clustered in three areas: informational approaches, behavioral and social approaches, and environmental and policy approaches. Informational approaches are designed to motivate, promote, and maintain behavior primarily by targeting cognition and knowledge about physical activity and its benefits. Behavioral and social approaches are designed to foster the development of behavioral management skills and modify the social environment to support changes in behavior. And environmental and policy approaches aim to increase opportunities to be physically active within the community. Ultimately, any policy or program aimed at increasing physical activity should recognize that fitness habits are the result of demographic (e.g., gender, age, ethnicity), psychological, lifestyle, and environmental factors. The decision to exercise and to maintain an exercise program often depends on a number of the factors, so an intervention with a single focus may not be as effective as a multifaceted approach.

Acknowledgments

This research was sponsored by the Air Force Resilience office and was led by Mr. Brian P. Borda for a significant portion of the study period and by Air Force Surgeon General Lt Gen (Dr.) Charles B. Green and Mr. William H. Booth, the Assistant Secretary of the Air Force for Manpower and Reserve Affairs (SAF/MRM).

We would like to thank the action officers from the sponsoring offices for their role in shaping the research agenda and providing feedback on interim and final briefings of the research findings. Those officers are Maj Kirby Bowling, our primary contact from the Air Force Resilience office; Col John Forbes and Lt Col David Dickey from the Air Force Surgeon General's office; and Linda Stephens-Jones from SAF/MRM. We also appreciate the insights and recommendations received from Ms. Eliza Nesmith while she was in the Air Force Services and from Lt Col Shawn Campbell while he served in the SAF/MRM office.

RAND's Sarah Meadows and Laura Miller led the overall research effort on resilience and provided extensive feedback on a previous draft of this manuscript. Donna White and Hosay Salam Yaqub provided valuable assistance formatting the manuscript and assembling the bibliography for publication.

Finally, we would like to thank Deborah Cohen and an anonymous reviewer for their feedback and guidance on improving the overall quality of this report.

Abbreviations

DHHS	Department of Health and Human Services
DoD	Department of Defense
IPAQ	International Physical Activity Questionnaire
TFF	Total Force Fitness

1. The Context of This Report[1]

This report is one of a series designed to support Air Force leaders in promoting resilience among Airmen, its civilian employees, and Air Force family members. The research sponsors requested that RAND assess the current resilience-related constructs and measures in the scientific literature and report any evidence of initiatives that promote resilience across a number of domains. We did not limit our search to research conducted in military settings or with military personnel, as Air Force leaders sought the potential opportunity to apply the results of these studies to a population that had not yet been addressed (i.e., Airmen). Further, many Air Force services support Air Force civilians and family members, and thus the results of civilian studies would apply to these populations.

This study adopts the Air Force definition of resilience: "the ability to withstand, recover and/or grow in the face of stressors and changing demands," which we found to encompass a range of definitions of resilience given throughout the scientific literature.[2] By focusing on resilience, the armed forces aim to expand their care to ensure the well-being of military personnel and their families through preventive measures and not by just treating members after they begin to experience negative outcomes (e.g., depression, anxiety, insomnia, substance abuse, post-traumatic stress disorder, or suicidal ideation).

Admiral Michael Mullen, Chairman of the Joint Chiefs of Staff from 2007 to 2011, outlined the Total Force Fitness (TFF) concept in a special issue of the journal *Military Medicine*: "A total force that has achieved total fitness is healthy, ready, and resilient; capable of meeting challenges and surviving threats" (Mullen, 2010, p. 1). This notion of "fitness" is directly related to the concept of resilience. The same issue of *Military Medicine* also reflected the collective effort of scholars, health professionals, and military personnel, who outlined eight domains of TFF: medical, nutritional, environmental, physical, social, spiritual, behavioral, and psychological. This framework expands on the traditional conceptualization of resilience by looking beyond the psychological realm to also emphasize the mind-body connection and the interdependence of each of the eight domains.

---

[1] Adapted from Meadows and Miller (forthcoming).

[2] The Air Force adopted this definition, which was developed by the Defense Centers of Excellence for Psychological Health and Traumatic Brain Injury (DCoE, 2011).

The research sponsors requested that RAND adopt these eight fitness domains as the organizing framework for our literature review. We followed this general framework, although in some cases we adapted the scope of a domain to better reflect the relevant research. Thus, this study resulted in eight reports, each focusing on resilience-related research in one of the TFF domains, but we note that not all of these domains are mutually exclusive. These eight reports define each domain and address the following interrelated topics:

- medical: preventive care, the presence and management of injuries, chronic conditions, and barriers and bridges to accessing appropriate quality health care (Shih, Meadows, and Martin, 2013)
- nutritional: food intake, dietary patterns and behavior, and the food environment (Flórez, Shih, and Martin, forthcoming)
- environmental: environmental stressors and potential workplace injuries and preventive and protective factors (Shih, Meadows, Mendeloff, and Bowling, forthcoming)
- physical: physical activity and fitness (Robson, 2013)
- social: social fitness and social support from family, friends, coworkers/unit members, neighbors, and cyber communities (McGene, 2013)
- spiritual: spiritual worldview, personal religious or spiritual practices and rituals, support from a spiritual community, and spiritual coping (Yeung and Martin, 2013)
- behavioral: health behaviors related to sleep and to drug, alcohol, and tobacco use (Robson and Salcedo, forthcoming)
- psychological: self-regulation, positive and negative affect, perceived control, self-efficacy, self-esteem, optimism, adaptability, self-awareness, and emotional intelligence (Robson, forthcoming).

These reports are not intended to be comprehensive reviews of the entire literature within a domain. Rather, they focus on those studies that consider the stress-buffering aspects of each domain, regardless of whether the term *resilience* is specifically used. This expanded the scope of the reviews to include a broader range of studies and also allowed for differences in the terminology used across different disciplines (e.g., stress management, hardiness). We sought evidence both on the main effects of resilience factors in each domain (i.e., those that promote general well-being) and on the indirect or interactive effects (i.e., those that buffer the negative effects of stress).

Because the Air Force commissioned this research to specifically address individuals' capacity to be resilient, and thus their well-being, our reports do not address whether or how fitness in each of the eight TFF domains could be linked to other outcomes of interest to the military, such as performance, military discipline, unit readiness, personnel costs, attrition, or retention. Those worthy topics were beyond the scope of this project.

Some other important parameters shaped this literature review. First, across the study, we focused on research from the past decade, although older studies are included, particularly landmark studies that still define the research landscape or where a particular line of inquiry has been dormant in recent years. Second, we prioritized research on adults in the United States. Research on children was included where particularly germane (e.g., in discussions of family as a form of social support), and, occasionally, research on adults in other Western nations is referenced or subsumed within a large study. Research on elderly populations was generally excluded. Third, we prioritized literature reviews, meta-analyses, and on-going bodies of research over more singular smaller-scale studies.

The search for evidence on ways to promote resilience in each domain included both actions that individuals could take and actions that organizations could take, such as information campaigns, policies, directives, programs, initiatives, facilities, or other resources. We did not filter out evidence related to Air Force practices already under way, as the Air Force was interested both in research related to existing practices and in research that might suggest new paths for promoting resilience. Our aim was not to collect examples of creative or promising initiatives at large but to seek scholarly publications assessing the stress-buffering capacity of initiatives. Thus, in general, this collection of reviews does not address initiatives that have not yet been evaluated for their effect.

Building on the foundation of the eight reports that assess the scientific literature in each domain, RAND prepared an overarching report that brings together the highlights of these reviews and examines their relevance to current Air Force metrics and programs. That ninth report, *Airman and Family Resilience: Lessons from the Scientific Literature,* provides a more in-depth introduction to resilience concepts and research, presents our model of the relationship between resilience and TFF, documents established and emerging Air Force resiliency efforts, and reviews the Air Force metrics for tracking the resiliency of Air Force personnel and their families. By comparing the information we found in the research literature to Air Force practices, we were able to provide recommendations to support the development of initiatives to promote resilience across the Air Force. Although the overview report contains Air Force-specific recommendations that take into account all eight domains and existing Air Force practices, some are applicable to the military more generally and are highlighted at the end of this report.

2. Physical Fitness Constructs, Measures, and Outcomes

"Lack of activity destroys the good condition of every human being, while movement and methodical physical exercise save it and preserve it."
— Plato, Philosopher

"It is exercise alone that supports the spirits, and keeps the mind in vigor."
— Marcus Tullius Cicero, Statesman

Few would challenge the importance of physical fitness and conditioning. Physical fitness contributes to health, in both mind and body, positively affects job performance, and is recognized as an essential requirement for Air Force readiness. Indeed, the Commander's Intent states:

> Being physically fit allows you to properly support the Air Force mission. The goal of the Fitness Program . . . is to motivate all members to participate in a year-round physical conditioning program that emphasizes total fitness, to include proper aerobic conditioning, strength/flexibility training, and healthy eating. Health benefits from an active lifestyle will increase productivity, optimize health, and decrease absenteeism while maintaining a higher level of readiness. Commanders and supervisors must incorporate fitness into the AF culture establishing an environment for members to maintain physical fitness and health to meet expeditionary mission requirements.
> — Department of the Air Force, 2012

This chapter will define physical fitness, describe common measures of physical fitness and physical activity, and then present an overview of the relationships between physical activity, health, well-being, and stress. We will conclude the chapter by reviewing the strategies and interventions for promoting physical activity and exercise.

Definition

As defined by the Department of Defense (DoD), physical fitness is "the capacity to perform physical exercise, consisting of the components of aerobic capacity, muscular strength, and muscular endurance in conjunction with body fat content within an optimal range" (Department of Defense, 2004). In compliance with this directive, the Air Force developed its standards for fitness using a composite overall fitness score and minimum scores in the areas of aerobic fitness, body composition, and muscular fitness. By integrating the DoD and Air Force definitions of fitness with broader definitions identified in the scientific literature, we defined physical fitness as a set of health- or performance-related attributes relating to the activities and condition of the body. This broader definition augments the DoD definition with the inclusion of physical activity. As discussed in more detail below, physical activity may be measured independently of physical fitness and can be a buffer against stress. However, we have excluded anthropometric (body composition) measures such as body mass index and hip-to-waist ratio.[3]

Physical Fitness and Activity Constructs

The physical fitness domain represents both physical activity and the physical abilities (fitness) that either facilitate the performance of physically demanding tasks or promote general health and well-being. Distinguishing health-related fitness from performance-related fitness is an important trend in physical fitness policy and research (Mood and Jackson, 2007; "Uniformed Health Services Profiles Programs," 2009). The primary objective of performance fitness tests is to determine an individual's physical capability. The time to complete a 50-yard dash is one example of a performance-related test. Standards for performance tests often correspond to normative data for gender and age, which are used to determine an individual's standing on underlying physical fitness and motor ability constructs. However, such constructs are developed to represent the full extent of physical abilities and are not necessarily linked to resilience or well-being.

More recently, the focus of research and policy has shifted to health-related fitness. The goal of health-related fitness is to identify and emphasize specific fitness constructs that are related to health outcomes (e.g., cardiovascular disease, obesity, osteoporosis). Using this approach, performance on fitness tests can be converted into risk scores for developing cardiovascular disease and other health-related outcomes. Consistent with our goal to promote resilience and well-being, we focus on health-related fitness rather than performance-related fitness constructs.[4]

---

[3] Those metrics, although relevant to physical fitness, are discussed in the companion report on the medical fitness domain (Shih, Meadows, and Martin, 2013).

[4] This is not to say that performance-related fitness is unimportant. On the contrary, it may be indirectly tied to resilience by optimizing human performance during physically and cognitively demanding missions.

Another important trend noted in our research is the distinction between physical fitness and physical activity (Mood and Jackson, 2007). Despite the relative ease of measuring the product of fitness (e.g., 50 situps in one minute), policy and research have redirected attention toward the process of physical activity ("Uniformed Health Services Profiles Programs," 2009; Mood and Jackson, 2007). Because both physical fitness and activity have sometimes been differentially linked to outcomes and have different dose-response relationships (Blair and Cheng, 2001), we will consider these as separate constructs.

Physical activity and physical fitness can be defined in a number of ways by identifying common underlying dimensions. Physical activity is generally classified by its mechanical or metabolic properties (Physical Activity Guidelines Advisory Committee Report, 2008). "Typically, mechanical classification stresses whether the muscle contraction produces movement of the limb: isometric (same length) or static exercise if there is no movement of the limb or isotonic (same tension) or dynamic exercise if there is movement of the limb. Metabolic classification involves the availability of oxygen for the contraction process and includes aerobic (oxygen available) or anaerobic (oxygen unavailable) processes. Whether an activity is aerobic or anaerobic depends primarily on its intensity" (U.S. Department of Health and Human Services, 1996, p. 20).

Although over 30 methods have been developed to measure physical activity and the associated mechanical or metabolic properties (Kriska and Caspersen, 1997; LaPorte, Montoye, and Caspersen, 1985), developing valid measurements has been a challenge (Montoye, 1984). Physical activity methods can be broadly categorized into objective (i.e., direct monitoring) or self-reported measures. These methods range in their acceptability to participants, cost, validity, and reliability. In general, precise objective measures have often been found to be impractical for use in population studies (LaPorte, Montoye, and Caspersen, 1985). Nonetheless, these measures may be particularly advantageous when determining the efficacy of an intervention.

Objective Measures

Objective methods of assessing physical activity include the use of calorimetry, heart rate monitors, gait assessment, pedometers, electronic motion sensor, accelerometers, and direct observation (see Table 1.1). Other methods available for measuring specific activities were not included as part of this review. For example, power meters and lap counters are specific to cycling and swimming, respectively. Although there are no accepted gold standards among the physical activity measures

Table 1.1. Objective Methods of Assessing Physical Activity

Measure	Description	Characteristics of Objective Measures			Limitations
		Expensive	Complex	Intrusive	
Indirect calorimetry	Provides an estimate of energy expenditure over a relatively short period of time by assessing oxygen consumption	X	X	X	Not suitable to measure patterns of physical activity
Heart rate monitor	Provides an estimate of intensity of activity or energy expenditure			X	Heart rate can be affected by factors other than activity (e.g., caffeine)
Pedometer	Measures number of steps taken by capturing vertical acceleration with a mechanical device				Limited to measurement of walking or jogging; does not capture intensity
Gait assessment	Measures both frequency of steps and force applied by means of an instrument inserted into shoe			X	Less widely used; validity unknown in population studies
Accelerometer/ electronic motion sensor	Measures velocity of the body over time with an electronic device typically attached to the hip or back		X		Less effective for measuring energy expenditure from certain activities (e.g., cycling)
Devices based on global positioning system (GPS)	Measures velocity and horizontal and vertical distance traveled				Research on validity of newer GPS devices is sparse
Cycling power meter	Measures power output, pedaling cadence, and velocity	X			Limited to cycling

(Tudor-Locke et al., 2004), many consider the doubly labeled water technique as one of the most direct methods of assessing activity (e.g., Sirard and Pate, 2001). This method measures CO^2 production, which is essentially an index of energy expenditure (Hill and Davies, 2007). The doubly labeled water technique has been used in some military samples (Forbes-Ewan et al., 1989), but it has far too many limitations to implement throughout the Air Force as a whole.

Some obvious limitations of using objective methods include the cost to implement, inconvenience to participants, and the requirement of specialized equipment or expertise. Other disadvantages, specific to particular methods, may include the need for individual calibration, variable quality of equipment, and lack of sensitivity to certain motions (e.g., Ward et al., 2005). Despite these limitations, objective measures are often used in smaller studies to offset social desirability and memory biases associated with self-reported measures.

Pedometers may be a viable option as an objective measure with relatively little administrative cost or burden on the participant. A review of studies evaluating the construct validity of pedometers indicates weak to moderate relationships to a range of fitness criteria, including body mass index, performance on a six-minute walk test, timed treadmill test, and estimated VO^2 max[5] (Tudor-Locke et al., 2004). Stronger evidence supporting the use of pedometers comes from a review evaluating convergent validity indicating strong positive associations between pedometers and time observed in activity (Tudor-Locke et al., 2004). Because pedometers were designed to capture vertical motion that occurs when walking or running, other popular activities such as cycling will not be measured accurately. Pedometers are further limited in their inability to capture the intensity of an activity. These limitations notwithstanding, pedometers offer a practical, low-cost method for objectively measuring physical activity.

Capturing a broader range of physical activity, accelerometers are more useful than pedometers because they can measure other important fitness dimensions (e.g., speed). Accelerometers have become widely available to the general public, as many cell phones contain accelerometers. Furthermore, many of these cell phones also come equipped with a GPS device, which further enhances the quality of the data to measure energy expenditure in a wide range of activities (e.g., cycling, kayaking). These devices are also relatively inexpensive and have been shown to be both valid and reliable measures of activity (Krenn et al., 2011; Ward et al., 2005). Additionally, these devices can often be paired with a heart rate monitor, which can then be used to estimate total energy expenditure. Overall, accelerometers and GPS devices are excellent options for objectively measuring physical activity for many populations.

However, pedometers and accelerometers may not be practical for some populations, such as children. Therefore, to assess the physical activity of children, researchers have advocated direct observation (e.g., Sirard and Pate, 2001). Direct observation measures use a variety of time-sampling approaches, such as partial, continuous, or momentary time sampling. These methods require that raters observe activity at a particular moment in time or for some specified period of time. The

---

[5] This is the maximum amount of oxygen the body can use during a specified period of usually intense exercise and depends on body weight and the strength of the lungs. It is commonly measured by increasing the intensity of exercise on a treadmill or cycle ergometer while measuring oxygen consumption.

available measures demonstrate acceptable validity and inter-rater agreement and can be used in a variety of settings.

Self-Reported Measures

Physical activity can be measured subjectively using a variety of methods including diaries, logs, and surveys. Although logs and diaries have been used to measure physical activity and can be valid measures, they are typically limited to a one- to three-day time span (Manley, 1999). Individuals must also demonstrate considerable commitment and effort to keep track of activities. Alternatively, surveys or questionnaires have been used to measure physical activity. Because questionnaires must often be tailored to target specific populations or to assess specific program goals, many different questionnaires have been developed. To organize reviews of these questionnaires, researchers have used several dimensions to guide their discussions. In an overview of physical activity questionnaires, Kriska and Caspersen (1997) differentiate questionnaires by an activity's attributes, including energy expenditure, complexity, time frame assessed, type of activity, reliability, and validity. In addition to using these dimensions, researchers also can compute an overall activity score from individuals' responses to a questionnaire, although they differ in how to make such computations. Although there are a number of different strategies, "[t]he two most common estimates . . . are derived from summing (1) time spent in physical activity; or (2) time weighted by an estimate of the intensity of that activity" (Kriska and Caspersen, 1997, p. 6)

In a more recent review of physical activity questionnaires, van Poppel et al. (2010) presented a rather dismal outlook. After reviewing 85 questionnaires, the authors found that research studies evaluating the measurement properties of these questionnaires were mostly of poor quality, preventing the recommendation of any one physical activity measure. The inconsistent quality of physical activity questionnaires has also been addressed in previous reviews (Kriska and Caspersen, 1997). However, at a minimum physical questionnaires should measure both the frequency and duration of activity and should give respondents the opportunity to indicate activity levels "in all settings (work, home, transport, recreation, sport) to have sufficient content validity" (p. 595). One very popular measure with promise is the L7S version of the International Physical Activity Questionnaire (IPAQ) (Bauman et al., 2009; Fogelholm et al., 2006; Levy and Readdy, 2004). The IPAQ has both a long and a short version and can be self-administered or by a researcher via telephone. The short-form (L7S) is suitable for monitoring population changes in activity levels, whereas the longer version is better designed for research applications.

Although we present examples of some widely used measures, self-reported measures, in general, are not recommended for tracking physical activity in the Air Force. As mentioned above, these measures typically provide unreliable and inaccurate reports of activity levels. Consequently, alternative methods that objectively measure physical activity (e.g., accelerometers) are recommended.

Physical Abilities (Fitness)

The dimensionality of physical fitness may depend, in part, on the goal of the research program. Specifically, some researchers have identified dimensions of physical fitness related to health promotion and others have examined job-relevant physical fitness dimensions. Despite these differences, the foundation to identify the basic structure of physical fitness has largely been attributed to Fleishman (1964). Fleishman's studies of Navy personnel suggested six underlying factors of physical fitness: explosive strength, gross body equilibrium, dynamic flexibility, balance with visual cues, extent of flexibility, and speed of limb movement. Although others have extended Fleishman's work (e.g., Baumgartner and Zuidema, 1972; Falls et al., 1965; Zuidema and Baumgartner, 1974), the most parsimonious taxonomy on the physical tasks in occupational settings suggests three underlying factors: strength, endurance, and movement quality (Hogan, 1991). This taxonomy, although developed for the study of job performance, is useful in a number of ways. First, these dimensions are easily differentiated and can be used to communicate job requirements and health benefits. They also provide a way to organize relevant metrics related to resiliency and readiness. Of course, identifying specific facets of these dimensions can broaden our understanding of the factors that prepare individuals for physically demanding jobs and promote positive health. For example, specific facets of movement quality may be important to the prevention of injuries; other facets are found to be less important.

A tremendous number of physical fitness tests have been developed to represent the various physical ability constructs. The majority of test development and research on fitness testing has been conducted on children, often within a school setting.[6] However, some common tests[7] used to determine fitness in adults include the one-mile walk, 1.5-mile run, the half situp test, pushups, and the sit-and-reach test. These and related tests are typically used to estimate an individuals' cardiorespiratory (i.e.,

---

[6] Military research has also contributed extensively to our knowledge of physical fitness.

[7] The Adult Fitness Test is part of the President's Challenge and was developed using a combination of tests from different sources including the YMCA and the Cooper Institute.

endurance) and muscular fitness. Many researchers argue that the best measure of cardiorespiratory fitness is maximal oxygen uptake, also known as VO^2 max (Manley, 1999). However, expensive equipment and trained technicians are required to accurately determine an individual's VO^2 max. These limitations have led to the development of methods and techniques to estimate VO^2 max from maximal and submaximal tests. Submaximal tests, which use heart rate to predict VO^2 max, are widely accepted, as they tend to reduce the burden on both the participant and the examiner (Manley, 1999). Submaximal tests require that participants perform some activity (e.g., cycle ergometer) at a level below their maximum effort. VO^2 is computed using the individual's performance (e.g., power output) and heart rate over a specified time period. Similar estimates of VO^2 max can also be determined by having individuals run for a specified time or distance

Muscular strength can be evaluated on all the major muscle groups. Common tests for muscular strength include "the bench press, leg extension, and biceps curl using free weights" (Manley, 1999, p. 34). Other popular tests, such as situps, pushups, and pullups, measure muscular endurance in addition to strength. Additionally, these particular tests are confounded by body weight (Knapik et al., 2004). That is, a larger individual must be stronger than a smaller individual to perform the same number of situps, pullups, or pushups. Consequently, tests requiring that individuals project, pull, or push their bodies are less standardized than tests using calibrated equipment.

Relatively few measures of flexibility have been developed and validated. The most widely known test of flexibility is the sit-and-reach test, which is a mostly a measure of flexibility in the hamstrings. Other tests developed for specific muscle groups have been developed (e.g., shoulder flex test) but have not received much attention from researchers.

Outcomes Related to Physical Activity and Fitness

There is a clear relationship between physical activity and health outcomes. As outlined in the President's Council on Physical Fitness and Sports (Booth and Chakravarthy, 2002), sedentary living (i.e., inactivity) increases the likelihood of many negative outcomes and chronic health conditions, including breast cancer, depression, hypertension, lower quality of life, and coronary artery disease. There are also large economic costs associated with physical inactivity (Colditz, 1999). There is also evidence that sitting for long periods may be a risk factor for adverse health outcomes, even when individuals participate in exercise (Hamilton et al., 2008). Consequently, researchers, health care practitioners, and government agencies continue to emphasize physical activity and exercise.

In 2009, the Department of Health and Human Services (DHHS) presented its physical activity guidelines for Americans. To create this report, DHHS conducted a comprehensive and exhaustive review of research examining the relationship between physical activity and physical and mental health. In general, their findings echo the conclusions of others (Garber et al., 2011; Salmon, 2001; Warburton, 206) "that frequent participation in physical activity was strongly linked to better health status throughout the life span" ("Physical Activity Guidelines Advisory Committee Reort," 2008, p. B-1). Furthermore, the data indicate that some exercise is better than no exercise and that health benefits accrue as exercise duration and intensity increase. However, the law of diminishing returns appears to apply to exercise time. That is, there is a progressive decline in the absolute health benefits accrued as exercise duration increases beyond a point. Overall, numerous research studies have led to the conclusion that each aspect of fitness (e.g., cardiorespiratory fitness, flexibility, muscular fitness) relates to one or more health outcomes (Garber et al., 2011). Rather than recapitulating the primary studies that support this conclusion, we present some additional important summary findings and recommendations from the DHHS report.

Physically active children and youth have higher levels of cardiorespiratory endurance and muscular strength than inactive young people, and well-documented health benefits include reduced body fat, more favorable cardiovascular and metabolic disease risk profiles, enhanced bone health, and reduced symptoms of anxiety and depression.

Strong evidence demonstrates that more active men and women have lower rates of all-cause mortality, coronary heart disease, high blood pressure, stroke, type 2 diabetes, metabolic syndrome, colon cancer, breast cancer, and depression. Strong evidence also supports the conclusion that more physically active adults and older adults exhibit a higher level of cardiorespiratory and muscular fitness, have a healthier body mass and composition, and have a biomarker profile that is more favorable for preventing cardiovascular disease and type 2 diabetes and for enhancing bone health. Modest evidence indicates that physically active adults and older adults have better sleep and health-related quality of life.

Strong evidence shows that physically active adults who are overweight or obese experience a variety of health benefits that are generally similar to those observed in people of optimal body weight (body mass index = 18.5–24.9). Some of the benefits appear to be independent of a loss in body weight, and in some cases, weight loss in conjunction with an increase in physical activity results in even greater benefits.

Strong evidence shows that a regimen of brisk walking provides a number of health and fitness benefits for adults and older adults, including lower risk of all-cause mortality, cardiovascular disease, and type 2 diabetes.

Regular physical exercise can also reduce sensitivity to and buffer against stress (Brown, 1991). Studies have shown that fitter individuals have decreased physiological reactivity (e.g., blood pressure) and demonstrate faster pulse rate recovery following exposure to stressors (cf. Brown, 1988). Furthermore, the adverse effects of stress have been shown to decrease when physical activity is increased over time (Brown, 1988). Consistent with this finding, some researchers have argued and found that physical activity, but not physical fitness, buffers against minor stresses (Carmack et al., 1999). The positive effects of exercise may function in part to stimulate important neurotrophic and neurogenic factors. Whereas stress decreases neurogenesis (i.e., development of neurons), exercise enhances neuronal functioning by facilitating the expression of certain neurotrophic and neurogenic factors, such as brain-derived neurotrophic factor. These factors support development of the nervous system, maintenance of neurons in the brain, and neural plasticity (Duman, 2005).

In general, the health benefits described in the previous sections can be seen in children who participate daily in at least 60 minutes of moderate to vigorous physical activity and in adults who are physically active for 30 to 60 minutes for at least five days per week ("Physical Activity Guidelines Advisory Committee Report," 2008). Consequently, significant health benefits can be accrued by participation in roughly two and a half to seven hours per week. Furthermore, the few studies that have examined the relationship between sex, racial and ethnic diversity, and these health benefits have not found any appreciable differences.

Although the evidence is clear that regular physical activity can promote physical health and can protect against the onset of certain mental health disorders and symptoms, including depression and anxiety, there are some identifiable risks associated with exercise. Disruption in regular patterns of exercise can elicit a range of negative emotions. For example, regular exercisers randomly assigned to an exercise withdrawal condition experienced increased levels of fatigue, depressive symptoms, and negative mood (Berlin, Kop, and Deuster, 2006). However, it should be noted that some researchers have raised concerns regarding the quality of studies examining the effects of exercise withdrawal (Szabo, 1998). Of particular concern is that individuals volunteering for exercise deprivation may be qualitatively different from the general population of regular exercisers.

Not all individuals who exercise will achieve immediate benefits. In fact, exercise may be unpleasant for some, especially individuals who have led a sedentary lifestyle (Salmon, 2001). Additionally, exercising at intensities beyond usual levels may deteriorate mood. Exercise, particularly running, can also lead to an increase in injuries (Koplan, Siscovick, and Goldbaum, 1985) and has been linked to an increased risk of sudden death, with the greatest risk to those who have been habitually inactive

(Thompson et al., 2007). Despite these legitimate concerns, the benefits from leading an active lifestyle far exceed the risks associated with a sedentary lifestyle.

Although clear guidelines have been developed for physical activity, specific standards for physical fitness tests have not been widely adopted. Whereas physical activity has broad benefits for the general population, ideal performance on physical fitness tests will depend heavily on gender, age, occupational requirements, and the desired health outcome. Consequently, fitness standards including those for the Air Force are generally scaled according to gender and age group, and additional standards may be set for specific occupations. Nevertheless, research has established a number of links between physical fitness tests and health-related outcomes. Research has shown that, in the military, low physical fitness is related to an increased risk of injuries in basic combat training (Knapik et al., 2004). In the general population, performance on endurance tests has been positively associated with better cardiovascular health (Blair and Cheng, 2001). Strength and movement quality tests (e.g., flexibility), on the other hand, have stronger associations with functional independence and injuries, particularly in older adults (Warburton, 2006). Strength training, also known as resistance training, promotes a healthy musculoskeletal system and prevents osteoporosis, sarcopenia, and low back pain (Winett and Carpinelli, 2001). Higher performance on strength tests has also been related to reduced injury and attrition rates and better performance on simulated tasks in the military (cf., Knapik et al., 2004). The benefits associated with resistance training can occur in just two short training sessions (15–20 minutes) each week incorporating each of the major muscle groups. Despite the benefits of strength training, test standards to determine optimal strength have not been determined.

Proponents of flexibility tests suggest that low flexibility may be a risk factor for certain ailments, such as low back pain (Hultman, Saraste, and Ohlsen, 1992). However, low back pain may be associated with many different factors, including psychosocial, socioeconomic, and physical factors (Andersson, 1999). Among these psychosocial factors are poor social support at work, low job satisfaction, poor working conditions, psychological distress, and depressive mood (Hartvigsen et al. , 2004; Hoogendoorn et al., 2000; Pincus et al., 2002). Although the literature on the health benefits of flexibility is not as extensive as it is for strength and endurance, the American College of Sports Medicine (ACSM) included recommendations for flexibility training to maintain a full range of motion with benefits accruing by engaging in flexibility exercises two to three days a week, while holding each stretch for 10–30 seconds (Garber et al., 2011). Furthermore, some limited evidence supporting the positive association with injuries was recently provided in a study of professional football players (Kiesel, Plisky, and Butler, 2011). However, Garber et al.

(2011) generally found that "no consistent link has been shown between regular flexibility exercise and a reduction of musculotendinous injuries, prevention of low back injury, or DOMS [delayed onset muscle soreness]" (p. 1344). Despite apparent inconsistent findings, the specific type and amount of flexibility needed will depend on both physical demands (i.e., occupational and recreational requirements) and individual factors, such as age (American College of Sports Medicine, 1998).

Summary Statement on Measures

Many different methods and techniques are available for measuring both physical activity and physical fitness. In general, physical fitness is more amenable to objective assessment. However, there are several concerns with the use of physical fitness measures to evaluate or promote resiliency programs. First, many factors affect performance on fitness exams beyond an individual's level of fitness. For example, pullups and situps will be more difficult for larger individuals, even if they are not fatter (Vanderburgh, 2008). Tests of cardiorespiratory fitness are also widely known to be affected by genetic inheritance (Manley, 1999; Salmon, 2001). These limitations lead us to agree with Blair and Cheng (2001) that "from a public health policy perspective, . . . recommendations and programs should be designed to promote physical activity and not fitness" (p. S397). Program goals and objectives should be carefully considered before selecting a measurement approach. For example, objective measures such as pedometers and accelerometers may be appropriate when evaluating relatively small interventions designed to promote ambulatory motion (e.g., walking, jogging, running). In contrast, questionnaires using self-report can be used for assessing population changes in physical activity but are generally limited by their inaccuracy and unreliability.

3. Interventions to Promote Physical Fitness

The promotion of physical activity has been explored from a number of perspectives. Consequently, several meta-analyses and reviews have been conducted examining a variety of interventions to promote physical activity. In fact, these reviews prompted the Health Development Agency in the United Kingdom to conduct an evidence briefing, a review of reviews, of public health interventions (Hillsdon, 2004). Varying levels of support were found for the different interventions, leading to three broad conclusions. First, brief interventions from health care professionals were found to generally result in short-term change in physical activity levels for those individuals who were previously sedentary. Second, interventions developed through community programs promoting home-based activity or participation in a fitness center showed good evidence for improving individual activity in both the short and long term. Examples of these interventions included weekly group meetings, telephone education and support, behavior modification (e.g., self-monitoring, reinforcement), and exercise testing and prescription. Finally, although workplace interventions remain a promising setting for interventions, sufficient data to draw conclusions are currently unavailable. Hillsdon (2004) concludes this review of reviews by noting the common attributes among effective interventions:

- "Individualised advice for behaviour change delivered verbally with written support;
- Setting goals for behaviour change;
- Self-monitoring;
- Explore cognitive and behavioural factors associated with behaviour change including beliefs about the costs and benefits of physical activity, reinforcement of changes in physical activity, perception of the health risks of physical inactivity, confidence to engage in physical activity;
- Ongoing verbal support;
- Intervention follow-up;
- Promote moderate intensity activity such as walking;
- Not dependent on attendance at a facility" (p. 22).

In a more structured review of physical activity interventions, Kahn et al. (2002) distinguished among three broad types of interventions: (1) informational approaches designed to motivate, promote, and maintain change, primarily by targeting cognitive skills, (2) behavioral and social approaches, which foster the development of behavioral management skills and modification of the social environment to support changes in behavior, and (3) environmental and policy approaches, which aim to increase opportunities for people to be physically active within their communities. Within these categories, the authors described and evaluated more specific interventions. Below, we briefly summarize the interventions most relevant to the Air Force community.[8]

For informational approaches, the available evidence suggests that point-of-decision prompts are relatively easy to implement and are effective in changing the target behavior. For example, these studies posted simple signs by elevators and escalators encouraging people to use the stairs. Another approach, requiring sufficiently greater resources and trained personnel, incorporates the use of community-wide campaigns. These efforts used communication techniques, through a wide range of media (e.g., television, radio, newspaper, billboards) to address sedentary behavior and the related risk factors for cardiovascular disease. Some form of social support (e.g., meetings, counseling) was also a key factor in these community campaigns. The available evidence indicates that these interventions can be effective in increasing physical activity, although the gains are small to moderate.

The second category of interventions, behavioral and social approaches, included interventions on family-based social support, social support in community settings, and health behavior change programs tailored to individuals. Although there was insufficient evidence to evaluate the effectiveness of family-based social support interventions, strong evidence was found for both social support programs in community settings and health behavior change programs. As the name implies, social support programs are designed to develop social networks that promote physical activity (e.g., walking groups). Health behavior change programs, designed specifically to match an individual's readiness to change and preferred activity, teach ways to integrate activity into daily routines. Several attributes are common among these interventions: "1) setting goals for physical activity and self-monitoring of progress toward goals, 2) building social support for new behavioral patterns, 3) behavioral reinforcement through self-reward and positive self-talk, 4) structured problem-solving geared to maintenance of the behavior change, and 5) prevention of relapse into sedentary behaviors" (Kahn et al., 2002, p. 85).

The final intervention category, environmental and policy approaches, attempts to increase opportunities for people to be physically active (e.g., access to fitness or community centers, walking trails). Many of these interventions also provided education to community members on a wide range of health-related behaviors. The

---

[8] Less-relevant interventions for the Air Force might include school-based physical education classes and college-based health education and physical education.

available evidence suggests that these interventions are also effective in increasing physical activity. Access and availability to exercise locations and facilities were also found to be central components related to physical activity (Humpel, Owen, and Leslie, 2002). This review also suggested that an environment's aesthetic qualities (e.g., friendly neighborhood, enjoyable scenery) may also have an effect on physical activity levels.

Although many of these reviews focused on the effectiveness of different interventions, few studies are available to guide policymakers on which programs are the most cost-effective. In response to this gap, Wu et al. (2011) provided a systematic review of the costs and benefits of different interventions. Their analysis suggests that although certain interventions (i.e., individually based programs) may be more effective at promoting physical activity, they can be less cost-effective than other interventions because they require more resources.

Other reviews have attempted to integrate research on increasing physical activity to reduce risks for specific outcomes. One such review focused on interventions targeting childhood obesity, including only studies that followed up for at least one year (Reilly and McDowell, 2003). Although their conclusions, that "there remains serious doubt as to the long-term efficacy, clinical relevance, and generalisability of published interventions in this area" (p. 615), are indeed grim, a focus on reducing sedentary behavior in obese children shows considerable promise. This approach emphasizes reinforcement for reducing sedentary behaviors that would otherwise compete with being physically active (e.g., watching television, playing on the computer, talking on the phone) (Epstein et al., 2000). It is also important to note that, as in many other studies, participants also received educational interventions for nutrition and diet. Nevertheless, this program showed considerable evidence of improvement in fitness levels and a corresponding reduction in weight.

In an attempt to reduce program costs, researchers continue to examine the effectiveness of low-cost interventions, such as telephone and web-based interventions for promoting physical activity. In a review of 16 studies, researchers found that telephone counseling interventions can be an effective way to promote physical activity (Eakin et al., 2007). More than two-thirds of the studies examined revealed positive effects, with stronger results for studies of longer duration and a higher volume of calls. However, it should be noted that studies in this meta-analysis most often used self-reported measures of activity as their outcome measure. As mentioned above, measures using self-report can be inaccurate and unreliable; therefore, additional studies using objective measures of physical activity (e.g., accelerometers) are needed.

Other cost-effective interventions, in their current state, are somewhat less promising. For example, a review of computer-tailored interventions, which provide individualized feedback to users, revealed that only three of the 11 studies examined had a positive effect on physical activity levels (Kroeze, Werkman, and Brug, 2006). Similarly disappointing findings were reported in a review of e-Health interventions, which is inclusive of a range of technology such as email, the Internet, CD-ROM programs, handheld computers, and kiosks. In this study, the authors found support for e-Health physical activity interventions for only three out of the 10 studies examined (Norman et al., 2007). Slightly better results were found in a review of studies evaluating website and email interventions. In this study, eight of the 15 studies reviewed showed improvement in physical activity (Vandelanotte et al., 2007). As in the studies on telephone interventions, stronger support was found when participants were contacted more than five times and the time to follow-up was short (i.e., less than three months). Although more research needs to be conducted on these technology-driven interventions, some evidence is available to suggest that Internet-based interventions are more effective than no interventions (van den Berg, Schoones, and Vlieland, 2007). Finally, emerging research suggests that interventions should also try to decrease sedentary behavior by promoting breaks or short periods of activity throughout the day. For example, individuals with more breaks from sedentary time (e.g., sitting) were found to have more positive health indicators, such as lower body mass index (Healy et al., 2008). This type of intervention may be particularly important for individuals who work long consecutive hours at their desks or computers, since sitting is considered a separate risk factor for adverse health outcomes (Hamilton et al., 2008).

Given the emphasis and evidence targeting physical activity, any successful intervention is likely to have incorporated key behavioral determinants in its design. These determinants were recently reviewed and categorized into individual and environmental characteristics that precede exercise (Sherwood and Jeffery, 2000). The individual characteristics included motivation, self-efficacy, stage of change, exercise history, body weight, health risk profiles, diet, and stress. Prominent among these factors are motivation, self-efficacy, and stress. Motivation is particularly important, since people start and continue to exercise for different reasons. Whether for fitness, health, social, personal achievement, or some other benefit, understanding the key motivators is central to promoting physical activity. Consequently, different forms of activity and programs may need to be supported to meet the various needs of the Air Force community. In addition to motivational factors, interventions must promote individual self-efficacy.[9] This belief and confidence in being able to engage in and overcome the barriers to physical activity "is the strongest and most consistent predictor of exercise behavior" among the psychological variables that have been studied (p. 25). These findings are consistent with guidelines in Garber et al. (2011), suggesting that moderate-intensity exercise rather than vigorous-intensity exercise may result in greater levels of participation and adherence, particularly among those new to regular exercise. Stress may also be an important factor affecting the motivation and maintenance of exercise. As discussed above, physical activity can buffer the adverse effects of stress; however, perceived stress can also disrupt exercise behavior. In a prospective study, researchers found that minor stress contributed to the omission of planned exercise sessions and reduced self-efficacy for future exercise (Stetson et al., 1997). Furthermore, when stressed, participants did not enjoy their exercise as much and overall were less satisfied with that week's exercise.

Environmental determinants of physical activity include social support, time, access, and injury (Sherwood and Jeffery, 2000). Among these variables, social support[10] is a key variable in both the initiation and maintenance of exercise, particularly among women. To effectively promote physical activity, individuals must perceive support from their families, friends, and the broader Air Force community (e.g., coworkers, unit leaders, supervisors). Social support may also be an important factor in exercise initiation following an injury. Injuries are fairly common among some forms of exercise. More specifically, as many as 20 to 50 percent of runners become injured (Buist et al., 2010; Buist et al., 2008; Jacobs and Berson, 1986), with the risks increasing for those who run frequently and who have previously been injured. Less research has been conducted on injury rates in other forms of exercise; however, some studies indicate that walking, gardening, swimming, bicycling, and hiking are associated with a lower risk of injury (Pons-Villanueva, Segui-Gomez, and Martinez-Gonzalez, 2010; Powell et al., 1998). More recent concerns in the military have been centered on the effects of popular extreme conditioning programs such as Cross Fit, which can be characterized by high-volume workouts with maximal efforts and minimal rest between efforts. There can be benefits to such training, but these programs are believed to increase the risk of musculoskeletal injury (Bergeron et al., 2011). In an effort to combat injuries related to physical training, Bullock et al. (2010)

---

[9] Self-efficacy is discussed in detail in the companion report on the psychological fitness domain (Robson, forthcoming).

[10] Social support is discussed in detail in the companion report on the social fitness domain (McGene, 2013).

review 40 physical training-related injury prevention strategies and found strong support for education of military leaders, leadership support, and unit injury surveillance as critical factors for developing a successful injury prevention program. Aside from injuries, perhaps the biggest barriers to the maintenance of exercise are real or perceived time constraints. With reductions in personnel, increases in missions, and conflicts with family obligations, the Air Force must ensure that exercise is not only established as a priority but is supported through policies, access to programs and facilities, and qualified personnel who can provide guidance and individualized feedback. These perceived barriers must be addressed to ensure that physical fitness is maintained both while at home station and while deployed.

4. Conclusion

This report has focused on the physical fitness domain of the Total Force Fitness construct. Physical fitness constructs can relate to either the ability to perform demanding physical tasks (performance-related fitness) or the promotion of general health and well-being (health-related fitness). Because of a recent shift in both research and policy, this chapter focused on health-related physical fitness. Specifically, it makes a distinction between physical *fitness* and physical *activity*. Physical fitness is a reflection of physical ability, whereas physical activity is characterized by biological, metabolic, and physical properties. Physical activity is viewed as a process.

Physical activity has many direct and indirect benefits to the health, well-being, and readiness of the force. It is strongly linked to better medical fitness (e.g., cardiorespiratory health, reduced risks for some cancers), physical fitness (e.g., body composition, muscular fitness), psychological fitness (e.g., stress-buffering, protection against depression and anxiety, increased self-esteem), and behavioral fitness (e.g., good sleep practices, sleep quality). Physical activity can also help reduce the major risks to optimal mission performance: physical injury, being overweight and psychosocial dysfunction. Furthermore, group physical activity can improve social fitness through the development of social networks and cohesion.

Efforts should be made to carefully evaluate the effectiveness of any physical fitness intervention, examining the activity needs across all demographic groups (e.g., gender, age, ethnicity, region). Evaluations should also distinguish between factors that influence the adoption of, maintenance of, and withdrawal from physical activity, since the factors driving a person to start exercising are likely to be very different from the reasons a person stops exercising (Sherwood and Jeffery, 2000). Research has shown that those who start an exercise program may have very different lifestyles, psychological resources, and physiological characteristics (Hooper and Veneziano, 1995). For example, individuals who smoked, experienced more stress at home, and were at a greater risk for cardiovascular disease were less likely to start exercising. To develop a sustainable program for the promotion of physical activity, it is important to recognize the role of these factors in the decisionmaking process of Airmen and their families. Understanding such motivational factors as physical appearance, weight loss, health benefits, and social benefits among others can help develop targeted messages and ensure that appropriate programs are developed to meet the community's needs.

In summary, the scientific evidence suggests that physical activity can promote fitness in at least five of the eight Total Force Fitness dimensions (i.e., psychological fitness, social fitness, behavioral fitness, medical fitness, and physical fitness) and can help to reduce risks to optimal mission performance. The contributions of physical fitness to resilience make it a smart investment, even in times of scarce resources.

Bibliography

American College of Sports Medicine Position Stand, "The Recommended Quantity and Quality of Exercise for Developing and Maintaining Cardiorespiratory and Muscular Fitness, and Flexibility in Healthy Adults," *Medicine and Science in Sports and Exercise*, Vol. 30, No. 6, June 1998, pp. 975–991.

Andersson, G., "Epidemiological Features of Chronic Low-Back Pain," *The Lancet*, Vol. 354, No. 9178, August 14, 1999, pp. 581–585.

Bauman, A., B. E. Ainsworth, F. Bull, C. L. Craig, M. Hagstromer, J. F. Sallis, M. Pratt, and M. Sjostrom, "Progress and Pitfalls in the Use of the International Physical Activity Questionnaire (IPAQ) for Adult Physical Activity Surveillance," *Journal of Physical Activity & Health*, Vol. 6, September 2009, pp. S5–S8.

Baumgartner, T. A., and M. A. Zuidema, "Factor Analysis of Physical Fitness Tests," *Research Quarterly*, Vol. 43, No. 4, December 1972, pp. 443–450.

Bergeron, M. F., B. C. Nindl, P. A. Deuster, N. Baumgartner, S. F. Kane, W. J. Kraemer, L. R. Sexauer, W. R. Thompson, and F. G. O'Connor, "Consortium for Health and Military Performance and American College of Sports Medicine Consensus Paper on Extreme Conditioning Programs in Military Personnel," *Current Sports Medicine Reports*, Vol. 10, No. 6, 2011, pp. 383–389. Doi 10.1249/Jsr.0b013e318237bf8a.

Berlin, A. A., W. J. Kop, and P. A. Deuster, "Depressive Mood Symptoms and Fatigue after Exercise Withdrawal: The Potential Role of Decreased Fitness," *Psychosomatic Medicine*, Vol. 68, No. 2, March–April 2006, pp. 224–230.

Blair, S. N., and Y. Cheng, "Is Physical Activity or Physical Fitness More Important in Defining Health Benefits?" *Medicine and Science in Sports and Exercise*, Vol. 33, No. 6 (Supplement), June 2001, pp. S379–S399; discussion S419-S420.

Booth, F. W., and M. V. Chakravarthy, "Cost and Consequences of Sedentary Living: New Battleground for an Old Enemy," *President's Council on Physical Fitness and Sports: Research Digest*, Vol. 3, No. 16, 2002, pp. 1–8.

Brown, J., "Exercise as a Buffer of Life Stress: A Prospective Study of Adolescent Health," *Health Psychology*, Vol. 7, No. 4, 1988, pp. 341–353.

Brown, J. D., "Staying Fit and Staying Well: Physical Fitness as a Moderator of Life Stress," *Journal of Personality and Social Psychology*, Vol. 60, No. 4, May 1991, pp. 555–561.

Buist, I., S. W. Bredeweg, K. A. Lemmink, W. van Mechelen, and R. L. Diercks, "Predictors of Running-Related Injuries in Novice Runners Enrolled in a Systematic Training Program: A Prospective Cohort Study," *The American Journal of Sports Medicine*, Vol. 38, No. 2, February 2010, pp. 273–280.

Buist, I., S. W. Bredeweg, W. van Mechelen, K. A. Lemmink, G. J. Pepping, and R. L. Diercks, "No Effect of a Graded Training Program on the Number of Running-Related Injuries in Novice Runners: A Randomized Controlled Trial," *The American Journal of Sports Medicine*, Vol. 36, No. 1, January 2008, pp. 33–39.

Bullock, S. H., B. H. Jones, J. Gilchrist, and S. W. Marshall, "Prevention of Physical Training-Related Injuries Recommendations for the Military and Other Active Populations Based on Expedited Systematic Reviews," *American Journal of Preventive Medicine*, Vol. 38, No. 1, 2010, pp. S156–S181. Doi 10.1016/J.Amepre.2009.10.023.

Carmack, C. L., E. Boudreaux, M. Amaral-Melendez, P. J. Brantley, and C. de Moor, "Aerobic Fitness and Leisure Physical Activity as Moderators of the Stress-Illness Relation," *Annals of Behavioral Medicine*, Vol. 21, No. 3, 1999, pp. 251–257.

Colditz, G. A., "Economic Costs of Obesity and Inactivity," *Medicine and Science in Sports and Exercise*, Vol. 31, No. 11, 1999, pp. S663–S667. Doi 10.1097/00005768-199911001-00026.

DCoE—*See* Defense Centers of Excellence.

Defense Centers of Excellence for Psychological Health and Traumatic Brain Injury (DCoE), *Traumatic Brain Injury,* 2011. As of April 9, 2011: http://www.dcoe.health.mil/

Department of the Air Force, "Air Force Guidance Memorandum for AFI 36-2905, Fitness Program," June 26, 2012.

Department of Defense, "DoD Physical Fitness and Body Fat Program," Directive 1308.1, June 30, 2004.

Duman, R. S., "Neurotrophic Factors and Regulation of Mood: Role of Exercise, Diet and Metabolism," *Neurobiology of Aging,* Vol. 26 (Supplement 1), December 2005, pp. 88–93.

Eakin, E. G., S. P. Lawler, C. Vandelanotte, and N. Owen, "Telephone Interventions for Physical Activity and Dietary Behavior Change: A Systematic Review," *American Journal of Preventive Medicine*, Vol. 32, No. 5, 2007, pp. 419–434.

Epstein, L. H., R. A. Paluch, C. C. Gordy, and J. Dorn, "Decreasing Sedentary Behaviors in Treating Pediatric Obesity," *Archives of Pediatrics and Adolescent Medicine*, Vol. 154, No. 3, 2000, pp. 220–226.

Falls, H. B., A. H. Ismail, D. F. MacLeod, J. E. Wiebers, J. E. Christian, and M. V. Kessler, "Development of Physical Fitness Test Batteries by Factor Analysis Techniques," *The Journal of Sports Medicine and Physical Fitness*, Vol. 5, No. 4, December 1965, pp. 185–197.

Fleishman, E. A., *The Structure and Measurement of Physical Fitness,* Englewood Cliffs, N.J.: Prentice-Hall, 1964.

Flórez, K. R., R. A. Shih, and M. T. Martin, *Nutritional Fitness and Resilience: A Review of Relevant Constructs, Measures, and Links to Well-Being,* Santa Monica, Calif.: RAND Corporation, RR-105-AF, forthcoming.

Fogelholm, M., J. Malmberg, J. Suni, M. Santtila, H. Kyrolainen, M. Mantysaari, and P. Oja, "International Physical Activity Questionnaire: Validity against Fitness," *Medicine and Science in Sports and Exercise*, Vol. 38, No. 4, April 2006, pp. 753–760.

Forbes-Ewan, C. H., B. L. Morrissey, G. C. Gregg, and D. R. Waters, "Use of Doubly Labeled Water Technique in Soldiers Training for Jungle Warfare," *Journal of Applied Physiology*, Vol. 67, No. 1, July 1989, pp. 14–18.

Garber, C. E., B. Blissmer, M. R. Deschenes, B. A. Franklin, M. J. Lamonte, I. M. Lee, D. C. Nieman, D. P. Swain, and American College of Sports Medicine, "Quantity and Quality of Exercise for Developing and Maintaining Cardiorespiratory, Musculoskeletal, and Neuromotor Fitness in Apparently Healthy Adults: Guidance for Prescribing Exercise," *Medicine and Science in Sports and Exercise*, Vol. 43, No. 7, 2011, pp. 1334–1359. Doi 10.1249/Mss.0b013e318213fefb.

Hamilton, M. T., G. N. Healy, D. W. Dunstan, T. W. Zderic, and N. Owen, "Too Little Exercise and Too Much Sitting: Inactivity Physiology and the Need for New Recommendations on Sedentary Behavior," *Current Cardiovascular Risk Reports*, Vol. 2, No. 4, 2008, pp. 292–298.

Hartvigsen, J., S. Lings, C. Leboeuf-Yde, and L. Bakketeig, "Psychosocial Factors at Work in Relation to Low Back Pain and Consequences of Low Back Pain; a Systematic, Critical Review of Prospective Cohort Studies," *Occupational and Environmental Medicine*, Vol. 61, No. 1, 2004, p. e2.

Healy, G. N., D. W. Dunstan, J. Salmon, E. Cerin, J. E. Shaw, P. Z. Zimmet, and N. Owen, "Breaks in Sedentary Time—Beneficial Associations with Metabolic Risk," *Diabetes Care*, Vol. 31, No. 4, 2008, pp. 661–666. Doi 10.2337/Dc07-2046.

Hill, R. J., and P. S. W. Davies, "The Validity of Self-Reported Energy Intake as Determined Using the Doubly Labelled Water Technique," *British Journal of Nutrition*, Vol. 85, No. 4, April 9, 2007, p. 415.

Hillsdon, M., "The Effectiveness of Public Health Interventions for Increasing Physical Activity Among Adults: A Review of Reviews: Evidence Briefing Summary," Health Development Agency, 2004.

Hogan, J., "Structure of Physical Performance in Occupational Tasks," *The Journal of Applied Psychology*, Vol. 76, No. 4, August 1991, pp. 495–507.

Hoogendoorn, W. E., M. N. M. van Poppel, P. M. Bongers, B. W. Koes, and L. M. Bouter, "Systematic Review of Psychosocial Factors at Work and Private Life as Risk Factors for Back Pain," *Spine*, Vol. 25, No. 16, 2000, p. 2114.

Hooper, J. M., and L. Veneziano, "Distinguishing Starters from Nonstarters in an Employee Physical Activity Incentive Program," *Health Education & Behavior*, Vol. 22, No. 1, 1995, p. 49.

Hultman, G., H. Saraste, and H. Ohlsen, "Anthropometry, Spinal Canal Width, and Flexibility of the Spine and Hamstring Muscles in 45-55-Year-Old Men with and without Low Back Pain," *Journal of Spinal Disorders*, Vol. 5, No. 3, September 1992, pp. 245–253.

Humpel, N., N. Owen, and E. Leslie, "Environmental Factors Associated with Adults' Participation in Physical Activity: A Review," *American Journal of Preventive Medicine*, Vol. 22, No. 3, April 2002, pp. 188–199.

Jacobs, S. J., and B. L. Berson, "Injuries to Runners: A Study of Entrants to a 10,000 Meter Race," *American Journal of Sports Medicine,* Vol. 14, No. 2, March–April 1986, pp. 151–155.

Kahn, E. B., L. T. Ramsey, R. C. Brownson, G. W. Heath, E. H. Howze, K. E. Powell, E. J. Stone, M. W. Rajab, and P. Corso, "The Effectiveness of Interventions to Increase Physical Activity," *American Journal of Preventive Medicine*, Vol. 22, No. 4S, 2002, pp. 73–107.

Kiesel, K., P. Plisky, and R. Butler, "Functional Movement Test Scores Improve Following a Standardized Off-Season Intervention Program in Professional Football Players," *Scandinavian Journal of Medicine & Science in Sports*, Vol. 21, No. 2, 2011, pp. 287–292.

Knapik, J. J., B. H. Jones, M. A. Sharp, S. Darakjy, S. Jones, and Army Center for Health Promotion and Preventive Medicine, "The Case for Pre-Enlistment Physical Fitness Testing: Research and Recommendations," Ft. Belvoir, Va.: Defense Technical Information Center, 2004.

Koplan, J. P., D. S. Siscovick, and G. M. Goldbaum, "The Risks of Exercise: A Public Health View of Injuries and Hazards," *Public Health Reports*, Vol. 100, No. 2, March 1985, pp. 189–195.

Krenn, P. J., S. Titze, P. Oja, A. Jones, and D. Ogilvie, "Use of Global Positioning Systems to Study Physical Activity and the Environment A Systematic Review," *American Journal of Preventive Medicine,* Vol. 41, No. 5, 2011, pp. 508–515. Doi 10.1016/J.Amepre.2011.06.046.

Kriska, A. M., and C. J. Caspersen, "Introduction to a Collection of Physical Activity Questionnaires," *Medicine and Science in Sports and Exercise,* Vol. 29, No. 6, March 23, 1997, pp. 5–9.

Kroeze, W., A. Werkman, and J. Brug, "A Systematic Review of Randomized Trials on the Effectiveness of Computer-Tailored Education on Physical Activity and Dietary Behaviors," *Annals of Behavioral Medicine,* Vol. 31, No. 3, 2006, pp. 205–223.

LaPorte, R. E., H. J. Montoye, and C. J. Caspersen, "Assessment of Physical Activity in Epidemiologic Research: Problems and Prospects," *Public Health Reports,* Vol. 100, No. 2, March–April 1985, p. 131.

Levy, S. S., and R. T. Readdy, "Reliability of the International Physical Activity Questionnaire in a Research Setting," *Research Quarterly for Exercise and Sport,* Vol. 75, No. 1, March 2004, pp. A40–A40.

Manley, A. F., "Historical Background, Terminology, Evolution of Recommendations, Physical Activity and Health: A Report of the Surgeon General," National Center for Chronic Disease Prevention and Health Promotion, 1999.

McGene, J., *Social Fitness and Resilience: A Review of Relevant Constructs, Measures, and Links to Well-Being,* Santa Monica, Calif.: RAND Corporation, RR-108-AF, 2013. As of October 2013:
http://www.rand.org/pubs/research_reports/RR108.html

Meadows, S. O., and L. L. Miller, *Airman and Family Resilience: Lessons from the Scientific Literature,* Santa Monica, Calif.: RAND Corporation, RR-106-AF, forthcoming.

Montoye, H. J., "Measurement of Physical Activity in Population Studies: A Review," *Human Biology; An International Record of Research,* 1984.

Mood, D. P., and A. W. Jackson, "Measurement of Physical Fitness and Physical Activity: Fifty Years of Change," *Measurement in Physical Education and Exercise Science,* Vol. 11, No. 4, 2007, pp. 217–227.

Mullen, Admiral M., "On Total Force Fitness in War and Peace," *Military Medicine,* Vol. 175 (Supplement), 2010, pp. 1–2.

Norman, G. J., M. F. Zabinski, M. A. Adams, D. E. Rosenberg, A. L. Yaroch, and A. A. Atienza, "A Review of Ehealth Interventions for Physical Activity and Dietary

Behavior Change," *American Journal of Preventive Medicine*, Vol. 33, No. 4, 2007, pp. 336–345. e316.

"Physical Activity Guidelines Advisory Committee Report to the Secretary of Health and Human Services, Part A: Executive Summary," *Nutrition Reviews*, Vol. 67, No. 2, February 2009, pp. 114–120.

Pincus, T., A. K. Burton, S. Vogel, and A. P. Field, "A Systematic Review of Psychological Factors as Predictors of Chronicity/Disability in Prospective Cohorts of Low Back Pain," *Spine*, Vol. 27, No. 5, 2002, p. E109.

Pons-Villanueva, J., M. Segui-Gomez, and M. A. Martinez-Gonzalez, "Risk of Injury According to Participation in Specific Physical Activities: A 6-Year Follow-up of 14 356 Participants of the Sun Cohort," *International Journal of Epidemiology*, Vol. 39, No. 2, April 2010, pp. 580–587.

Powell, K. E., G. W. Heath, M. J. Kresnow, J. J. Sacks, and C. M. Branche, "Injury Rates from Walking, Gardening, Weightlifting, Outdoor Bicycling, and Aerobics," *Medicine and Science in Sports and Exercise*, Vol. 30, No. 8, August 1998, pp. 1246–1249.

Reilly, J. J., and Z. C. McDowell, "Physical Activity Interventions in the Prevention and Treatment of Paediatric Obesity: Systematic Review and Critical Appraisal," *Proceedings of the Nutrition Society*, Vol. 62, No. 3, 2003, pp. 611–619.

Robson, S., *Physical Fitness and Resilience: A Review of Relevant Constructs, Measures, and Links to Well-Being,* Santa Monica, Calif.: RAND Corporation, RR-104-AF, 2013. As of October 2013:
http://www.rand.org/pubs/research_reports/RR104.html

———, *Psychological Fitness and Resilience: A Review of Relevant Constructs, Measures, and Links to Well-Being,* Santa Monica, Calif.: RAND Corporation, RR-102-AF, forthcoming.

Robson, S., and N. Salcedo, *Behavioral Fitness and Resilience: A Review of Relevant Constructs, Measures, and Links to Well-Being,* Santa Monica, Calif.: RAND Corporation RR-103-AF, forthcoming.

Salmon, P., "Effects of Physical Exercise on Anxiety, Depression, and Sensitivity to Stress: A Unifying Theory," *Clinical Psychology Review*, Vol. 21, No. 1, March 2001, pp. 33–61.

Sherwood, N. E., and R. W. Jeffery, "The Behavioral Determinants of Exercise: Implications for Physical Activity Interventions," *Annual Review of Nutrition*, Vol. 20, No. 1, 2000, pp. 21–44.

Shih, R. A., S. O. Meadows, and M. T. Martin, *Medical Fitness and Resilience: A Review of Relevant Constructs, Measures, and Links to Well-Being,* Santa Monica, Calif.: RAND Corporation, RR-107-AF, 2013. As of October 2013: http://www.rand.org/pubs/research_reports/RR107.html

Shih, R. A., S. O. Meadows, J. Mendeloff, and K. Bowling, *Environmental Fitness and Resilience: A Review of Relevant Constructs, Measures, and Links to Well-Being,* Santa Monica, Calif.: RAND Corporation, RR-101-AF, forthcoming.

Sirard, J. R., and R. R. Pate, "Physical Activity Assessment in Children and Adolescents," *Sports Medicine* (Auckland, N.Z.), Vol. 31, No. 6, 2001, pp. 439–454.

Stetson, B. A., J. M. Rahn, P. M. Dubbert, B. I. Wilner, and M. G. Mercury, "Prospective Evaluation of the Effects of Stress on Exercise Adherence in Community-Residing Women," *Health Psychology,* Vol. 16, No. 6, November 1997, pp. 515–520.

Szabo, A., "Studying the Psychological Impact of Exercise Deprivation: Are Experimental Studies Hopeless?" *Journal of Sport Behavior,* Vol. 21, No. 2, 1998, pp. 139–147.

Thompson, P. D., B. A. Franklin, G. J. Balady, S. N. Blair, D. Corrado, N. A. Estes III, J. E. Fulton, N. F. Gordon, W. L. Haskell, M. S. Link, B. J. Maron, M. A. Mittleman, A. Pelliccia, N. K. Wenger, S. N. Willich, and F. Costa, "Exercise and Acute Cardiovascular Events Placing the Risks into Perspective: A Scientific Statement from the American Heart Association Council on Nutrition, Physical Activity, and Metabolism and the Council on Clinical Cardiology," *Circulation,* Vol. 115, No. 17, May 1, 2007, pp. 2358–2368.

Tudor-Locke, C., J. E. Williams, J. P. Reis, and D. Pluto, "Utility of Pedometers for Assessing Physical Activity: Construct Validity," *Sports Medicine,* Vol. 34, No. 5, 2004, pp. 281–291.

"Uniformed Health Services Profiles Programs," December 3, 2009, pp. 1–28.

U.S. Department of Health and Human Services, Centers for Disease Control and Prevention, National Center for Chronic Disease Prevention and Health Promotion, *Activity and Health: A Report of the Surgeon General,* Atlanta, Ga., 1996.

van den Berg, M. H., J. W. Schoones, and T. P. M. V. Vlieland, "Internet-Based Physical Activity Interventions: A Systematic Review of the Literature," *Journal of Medical Internet Research,* Vol. 9, No. 3, 2007.

van Poppel, M. N. M., M. J. M. Chinapaw, L. B. Mokkink, W. van Mechelen, and C. B. Terwee, "Physical Activity Questionnaires for Adults: A Systematic Review of Measurement Properties," *Sports Medicine* (Auckland, N.Z.), Vol. 40, No. 7, July 1, 2010, pp. 565–600.

Vandelanotte, C., K. M. Spathonis, E. G. Eakin, and N. Owen, "Website-Delivered Physical Activity Interventions: A Review of the Literature," *American Journal of Preventive Medicine*, Vol. 33, No. 1, 2007, pp. 54–64.

Vanderburgh, P. M., "Occupational Relevance and Body Mass Bias in Military Physical Fitness Tests," *Medicine & Science in Sports & Exercise*, Vol. 40, No. 8, 2008, pp. 1538–1545.

Warburton, D. E. R., "Health Benefits of Physical Activity: The Evidence," *Canadian Medical Association Journal*, Vol. 174, No. 6, April 14, 2006, pp. 801–809.

Ward, D. S., K. R. Evenson, A. Vaughn, A. B. Rodgers, and R. P. Troiano, "Accelerometer Use in Physical Activity: Best Practices and Research Recommendations," *Medicine & Science in Sports & Exercise*, Vol. 37, No. 11 (Supplement), 2005, pp. S582–S588.

Winett, R. A., and R. N. Carpinelli, "Potential Health-Related Benefits of Resistance Training," *Preventive Medicine*, Vol. 33, No. 5, November 2001, pp. 503–513.

Wu, S. Y., D. Cohen, Y. Y. Shi, M. Pearson, and R. Sturm, "Economic Analysis of Physical Activity Interventions," *American Journal of Preventive Medicine*, Vol. 40, No. 2, 2011, pp. 149–158. Doi 10.1016/J.Amepre.2010.10.029.

Yeung, D., and M. T. Martin, *Spiritual Fitness and Resilience: A Review of Relevant Constructs, Measures, and Links to Well-Being,* Santa Monica, Calif.: RAND Corporation, RR-100-AF, 2013. As of October 2013: http://www.rand.org/pubs/research_reports/RR100.html

Zuidema, M. A., and T. A. Baumgartner, "Second Factor Analysis Study of Physical Fitness Tests," *Research Quarterly*, Vol. 45, No. 3, October 1974, pp. 247–256.

Made in the USA
Middletown, DE
02 August 2021